Bible Stories

Enid Blyton

It's wonderful to see that Enid Blyton's inspirational writing is being made available to today's young readers.

Her writing style has the same richness of language that can be found in the King James version of the Bible, so new readers will be treated to not only good stories but her "poetry in voice" as well.

Tomie dePaola

Bible Stories

Enid Blyton

Illustrated by Liz Pichon

ELEMENT
CHILDREN'S BOOKS

SHAFTESBURY, DORSET · BOSTON, MASSACHUSETTS · MELBOURNE, VICTORIA

Enid Blyton

Text © Enid Blyton Limited 1955
All Rights Reserved

Enid Blyton's signature is a trademark of Enid Blyton Limited
For further information please contact www.blyton.com

First published in Great Britain by Frederick Muller in 1955
First published by Element Children's Books in 1998,
Shaftesbury, Dorset SP7 8BP
Published in the USA in 1998 by Element Books Inc.
160 North Washington Street, Boston MA 02114

Published in Australia in 1998 by Element Books Limited
and distributed by Penguin Books Australia Ltd,
487 Maroondah Highway, Ringwood, Victoria 3134

British Library Cataloguing in Publication data available.

Library of Congress Cataloging in Publication data available.

ISBN 1 901881 42 3

Cover design by Gabrielle Morton

Cover and inside illustrations © Liz Pichon 1998

Typeset by Dorchester Typesetting Group Ltd
Printed and bound in Great Britain by Creative Print and Design

Other titles by Enid Blyton
published by
Element Children's Books

Knights of the Round Table
Tales of Ancient Greece
Robin Hood Book
Tales from the Arabian Nights
The Land of Far-Beyond
The First Christmas
A Story Book of Jesus

Foreword for the Child

The greatest book in the world is the Bible. In it are hundreds of stories you should know – great stories that you will want to read again and again, and will never forget.

But the Bible is a very big book, and not always easy for a small child to read – so I have chosen a few stories for you myself, and retold them in this little book. Later on you will be able to read them in the Bible itself, with many, many others.

The Bible is in two parts, called the Old Testament and the New Testament. I have chosen four stories from the Old and five from the New. They are:

The First Noah's Ark
The Baby in the Bulrushes
Daniel in the Lion's Den
David and the Giant
and
The Night the Angels Came
When Jesus Was a Child
Satan Comes to Jesus
Jesus Begins his Work
A Little Boy Who Was Ill

I hope you will like these stories so much that you will want to read the Bible yourself as soon as you can.

Enid Blyton

Stories from the Old Testament

The First Noah's Ark

Listen while I tell you the story of the first Noah's Ark.

Long, long ago there was a time when the world was full of wicked people, and God, our heavenly father, was sad when He looked down on the earth, and saw so much cruelty and greed and hatred.

"I must make an end to such wickedness," said God. "I shall send a great flood upon the earth – but there is one man I will save, and that is the good man, Noah. He and all his family shall be saved."

Noah was the only good man among all the wicked ones. He would not do the things they did, but lived apart with his family, doing good instead of evil.

One day God came to Noah and spoke to him. "Soon a great flood of water will come over the earth, and the wicked people will be swept away. But you and your family shall be saved."

"How may we be saved?" asked Noah, in wonder.

"You must make yourself an ark, a ship that will float on the water," said God. "You must make rooms inside, and daub them with pitch to keep out the water and the rain."

So Noah made an ark, a great ship that would float well on water. He and his three sons, Shem, Ham, and Japheth, cut down trees, and sawed and hammered day after day.

Many people came to watch what Noah was doing, and they laughed at him.

"Why do you build a ship on dry land?" they said. "You are mad! And why do you make such an enormous one? It is far too big for you and your family."

Noah was building the Ark for others beside himself. God had told him that he was to take with him into the Ark two of every living creature. A very big ship was needed to hold so many.

One day Noah called to him two of every animal, bird, and insect. He opened the door of the great Ark, and all the animals went in two by two. Noah put in food as well, for he would need plenty to feed his family and all the creatures too.

Then Noah and all his family went into the Ark, and the great door was shut. Noah went fearfully to the window and gazed out. What was happening to the weather? It had been very strange for the last few days.

The skies were dark, great winds blew, and clouds of dust swept around the Ark. Then, as Noah watched, it seemed to him as if the skies suddenly opened and a great torrent of water fell down on the world.

So the great rains began. Day after day there was the noise of rain hammering on the roof, and of a great wind that roared all around. Thunder rolled and lightning flashed from the angry skies.

Everyone on the earth was full of fear. What was happening? The storms grew fiercer, and the rain fell down

all day and all night without stopping. Water ran everywhere, and great floods began to sweep over the land.

Noah felt the Ark move as water swept against it. It was afloat! The floods were bearing it along like a ship. Now Noah knew why God had commanded him to make such a big strong Ark. It was the only thing that would save anyone from the heaving waters.

For days the rain fell, for forty days, and forty nights! Always the people in the Ark could hear the noise of the raindrops on the roof, and the howling of the great wind. The Ark swayed from side to side as the wind made waves on the floods, and at first Noah's family were afraid.

But the Ark was strong and kept them all safe, and

soon everyone grew used to the rain and wind, and went about their work in peace. There was much to do – the animals had to be fed, and every corner of the great ship had to be watched for leaks. Noah trusted in God and knew that the day would come when the world would once again be fit to live in.

Noah looked out of the one window in the Ark. What a strange and gloomy world he saw. "It is all grey water, grey rain, grey mists!" he said. "How I long to see the golden sun!"

And then, after forty days and forty nights there came a change in the sounds outside the Ark.

"The rain is not so heavy," said Noah, "and the wind does not howl so loudly. And see, surely there is a light behind the clouds, as if the sun would once more shine!"

How glad everyone was! The birds sang in the Ark, and the animals lifted their heads joyfully. The children ran about and chattered in delight.

Noah looked from the window again. The mists were clearing away at last – and suddenly the sun shone out, warm and golden. What a wonderful sight after so many grey days of storm and rain!

But what a strange world the sun shone down on – nothing but water! No land was to be seen anywhere, not even the highest mountain-top, for the floods

covered everything. Far down below the deep, heaving waters lay a drowned world. Only the good man Noah, and all his family, were safe, as God had meant them to be.

The waters began to go down, and at last Noah saw a mountain-top gleaming in the sunshine. Soon the Ark came to rest on the top of a high mountain called Ararat, and presently, all around, the tops of other mountains appeared.

Noah took a raven and set the big black bird free in the warm air. It flew away in delight, and did not come back, but flew to and fro over the waters.

Then Noah took a dove and set her free, but she came back because she could not find anywhere to rest the sole of the foot. "There cannot be much land showing yet," said Noah. "I will send her out again in a week."

So he did, and this time, when she came back, she carried an olive leaf in her beak. "See!" said Noah to his family, "the tops of trees must be above the waters now. Next time we free the dove she will not come back."

He was right. The dove found plenty of trees to roost in when Noah set her free for the third time. The floods had gone! Noah and his sons took off the roof of the Ark, and rejoiced to feel the sun and the breeze.

And then Noah told his sons to free all the animals caged in the Ark. How they longed to get out into the sunshine!

What a wonderful day that was when at last every one could go forth from the Ark, and walk on dry land once more. How they shouted and sang!

"I shall immediately build an altar," said Noah, "and thank God for saving us from the floods."

Then, as Noah prayed at the altar he had built, the voice of God came to him, with a solemn promise.

"Never again shall there come a great flood like this," said God. "See – as a token of my promise I will set a bow in the clouds, so that all who see it may remember my words."

And then Noah saw a wondrous thing. A great shimmering bow appeared in the sky, a magnificent arch of many colors. It hung there, far above Noah's head, the most beautiful thing he had ever seen.

It was a rainbow. When you see it in the sky you will remember God's promise made so very very long ago.

The Baby in the Bulrushes

Once upon a time, long ago, there lived a cruel king called Pharaoh. He had may slaves who worked hard for him all day long in the hot sun.

Pharaoh was afraid of the slaves. "There are too many of them," he said. "Soon there will be more slaves than soldiers! They have too many children also, and I must think of a way to prevent such a thing."

So he gave a very cruel command. "Take every boy-baby away from his mother, and throw him into the river Nile," he said. "Then there will not be so many of these slaves!"

The poor slave-mothers wept bitterly when they heard this. They loved their little sons, and they hated Pharaoh for his cruelty.

Now there was one mother called Jochabed. She had a beautiful little baby boy, and she could not bear to think that soldiers might come to take him away. How could she save her little son?

At last she thought of a plan, and she called her little daughter Miriam to her and told her the secret. Together they made a little ark, a basket, from the bulrushes in the river. They daubed it with slime and pitch, so that no water could seep through, and they put a blanket inside.

"And now we will hide our baby among the reeds quite near to the place where the princess comes to bathe in the mornings," said Jochabed. "Come, Miriam!"

Miriam hid the little floating basket among the bulrushes, and waited nearby. Early in the morning

Pharaoh's lovely daughter came down with her maids to bathe in the river. Miriam peeped through the bulrushes and saw her.

"I will take my bath now," said the princess, and then suddenly she caught sight of something in the reeds.

"What is that floating on the water?" she said. "It is a little boat made of rushes! What does it hold?"

"I will fetch it for you," said one of her maids, and waded out to the little ark.

The little maid fetched the ark of bulrushes and took it to the princess. "It is heavy," she said. "What *can* be inside?"

The princess lifted up the lid – and inside was the lovely baby, still fast asleep. He woke up suddenly, and began to cry in fright.

"Oh, what a beautiful baby!" said the princess, in delight. "Let me hold you, little one! Don't cry, you are safe!"

She held the baby lovingly, and rocked him to and fro, talking to him. He stopped crying and looked up at her with a sudden smile.

The princess held him tightly, and smiled down at him. "This must be a baby belonging to one of the slaves," she said. "I cannot have him thrown into the river. I love him, he is beautiful."

Miriam watched all that happened from her hiding-place in the reeds.

"Oh! The princess loves our baby!" she said, and she crept out shyly and went to the beautiful maiden who was cradling the baby so lovingly in her arms.

"Would you like a nurse for the baby?" she said. "Shall I fetch one of the slaves – I know one who would be glad to nurse the child for you, and look after him."

The baby smiled up at the princess again, and she wished he were her own. Yes – she *must* keep him! She looked down at the kneeling Miriam.

"You may go and fetch someone who will nurse this child for me," she said. "Someone kind, who will love him."

Miriam's heart leapt for joy. Her dear little brother was saved!

She ran off at once to her mother, her eyes shining. "Mother!" she cried. "Oh, Mother! The princess found our little baby in his ark of bulrushes! She took him into her arms, she loved him. He smiled up at her and she said, 'He is beautiful!'"

"Now God be praised!" said Jochabed. "What is the princess going to do with my little son, Miriam?"

"She has taken him to the palace," said Miriam. "But, Mother – *you* are to be his nurse! Quick, come with me – we will go to the palace and speak with the princess there!"

Jochabed hurried away with Miriam to the palace, and a servant took them to the princess. She sat holding the sleeping baby against her shoulder.

"I have brought a nurse for the baby," said Miriam shyly, kneeling behind her mother.

The princess was pleased to see this kindly slave-woman. "See," she said, "I found this baby in the bulrushes. I love him, and when he is old enough I shall make him my own son. But now I want a nurse for him.

Will you take him for me? I will pay you wages, and when he is grown, you shall bring him to me at the palace, and he shall be a little prince."

Jochabed wept tears of joy as she took her little son from the princess. Now their baby was safe; he would go back to his own home and grow up with his own family.

The princess gave the baby a kiss. She guessed that Jochabed was his own mother, and she was glad that she had saved such a beautiful child. Now he would be loved and cherished!

"His name shall be Moses," she said, "because 'Moses' means 'Taken from the Water.' It is a good name for him."

So little Moses was taken home by his mother, with Miriam running happily beside them. Now he did not need to be hidden away, but could grow up safely and happily.

"You are mine again, little baby-in-the-bulrushes!"

said his mother. "And you shall be mine till you are grown – and then I will take you to the palace, and you will be a little prince!"

How the baby chuckled and laughed. He did not understand a word – but he knew well enough that he was in his mother's arms and that she was happy!

Daniel in the Lion's Den

This is the story of a brave man.

His name was Daniel, and he was a slave. King Darius of Babylon had captured him and had brought him to his own country to work for him. Daniel was clever and he could be trusted. The king liked him, and as the years went by he raised up the slave and made him a prince. He talked often with Daniel, and asked his advice, and he gave him many presents.

The other princes were very jealous. "This man Daniel was once a slave," they said. "Now see, he is at the king's right hand and gives him advice on all things. He has many gifts from Darius, far more than we have."

"Some day he will do wrong," said one of the princes. "Then our chance will come; we will tell the king and Daniel will be punished."

But Daniel was a good man. No matter how the princes watched him they could not find him doing any wrong thing.

The princes talked among themselves again. "I have thought of a way to turn the king against Daniel," said one. "You know that he does not worship our idols as we do, and will not bow down before them. Instead he prays to his own God, and says that our idols are false."

"That is true," said another prince. "I have watched him open his windows towards Jerusalem, where he was born, three times each day, and pray to his God."

"Now here is my plan," said the first prince. "We will go to the king, and beg him to make a new law. And that law shall be that no one shall pray to anyone except to the king himself for thirty days!"

"And Daniel will not obey – he will still go on praying to his own God!" said the others. "Then we will tell the king, and Daniel shall be put to death!"

So they went to the king. "O great Lord," said the princes, "command that no one shall pray to anyone but you for thirty days!"

"I will do so," said King Darius, and he signed a decree that was sent throughout the land. "If anyone disobeys, he shall be cast into the den of lions," said the king.

Everyone but Daniel obeyed the king's command. Daniel was not going to stop praying to God, so, as he always did, he opened his window three times a day

towards Jerusalem, and each time he prayed to his God.

The jealous princes watched, and went at once to the king. "Lord," they said, "you have said that anyone who disobeys your command shall be thrown to the lions, but Daniel opens his windows three times a day and prays to his God and not to you."

The king looked in anger at the princes, but his face was sad. He knew at once that they had tricked him, so that they might do harm to the man they hated. He dismissed the princes and sat alone, thinking.

"Why did I command such a foolish thing?" he thought. "I cannot have my favorite prince put to death." But although the king sat thinking all the day he could not see any way of saving Daniel from death. In the evening the princes came to him again.

"Lord," they said, "your command must be obeyed – not even a king can alter a decree once it has been made."

Darius looked at the princes sadly. "I know this well," he said. "Bring Daniel before me. He shall be thrown into the den of lions."

Daniel was brought before Darius and stood there silently. He had been told what was to happen to him.

"Daniel," said Darius, "may the God to whom you pray each day save you from the lions!"

Then men took hold of Daniel and flung him into the great pit where the fierce lions raged all day long. They put a heavy stone over the entrance to the den, and the

king sealed the stone with his royal seal.

All that night the king was sad. He tossed and turned on his couch, thinking of Daniel with the savage lions. He tried to sleep but he could not.

"He was my trusted friend," thought Darius. "He was wise and good. Now I have sent him to his death because of the jealousy of the other princes."

Early in the morning the king rose from his bed and went out into the dawn. He stood beside the stone that sealed the entrance to the den.

"O Daniel, Daniel!" cried the king, in sorrow, "Daniel, servant of God! Was your God able to save you from the lions?"

The king did not expect any answer from the pit – but, to his great amazement, a loud, clear voice called up from below.

"O King, your servant is here. In the night there came an angel from the Lord my God. He shut the mouths of the lions, and not one of them has hurt me."

The king listened, hardly able to believe that Daniel was alive and unhurt. Then he shouted for his servants, and they came running to him. "Take away this stone and bring up Daniel, my prince, from the lions' den!" he commanded.

The stone was rolled away, and the astonished

servants peered down into the pit. There stood Daniel quite unhurt among the lions.

The servants pulled him up into the sunshine, and he

stood there, unharmed, with not a mark upon his body. The king rejoiced to see him.

"Now will I make a *new* decree, Daniel!" he said. "I will tell everyone in my kingdom that they must fear the God of Daniel, who delivers and saves those who love him, and whose signs and wonders are worked in heaven and earth."

So King Darius signed another decree, and sent it through the land. The people read it and marveled.

"The God of Daniel is the true God and remains steadfast for ever!" they said.

And so, because of one brave man, the people turned from their idols, and prayed to the true God, who had sent his angel to save Daniel from the lions raging in their den.

David and the Giant

Davvid was a little shepherd boy who looked after his father's sheep. One day his brothers told him that they were going away to fight.

"We have to fight the Philistines, who are our enemies," said his brothers. "We shall want food at times, David, and then you must leave your sheep, and bring us bread and cheese."

His brothers all went away to fight. Soon they sent word that they needed food, and David left his father's sheep and went over the hills to find his brothers. He felt excited – perhaps now he would see a battle!

He came to his brothers' camp and gave them the food. As he spoke with them, a most surprising thing happened.

A giant marched out of the enemy's camp, an enormous fellow, tall and burly and very strong. He was dressed in a coat of mail and wore a great shining helmet of brass. His servant, carrying his master's shield, strode in front of him.

As David watched in amazement, the giant, whose name was Goliath, began to shout in his enormously loud voice.

"Bring me a man to fight with! If he is strong enough to kill me, then the Philistines, your enemy, shall be your servants. But if I kill him, then you shall be our men and serve us! Have you no brave men in your army to send against me this day?"

David saw that many men in his brothers' camp ran away when the giant appeared. Not one went to fight him, for they were all much too afraid.

"Will no one go to fight this giant?" said David.

"We fear him," said his brothers. "He has mocked us like this for forty days."

"*I* will fight him!" said David.

Now King Saul, who was the captain of the camp, heard him and laughed. "You are only a boy!" he said. "This man has fought in battle for years!"

"I have killed a lion and I have killed a bear," said David. "The Lord God will help me against this giant."

"You shall fight him then!" said the king, and sent for armor to put on David. The boy pulled on a coat of mail and a great helmet, and wore an enormous sword at his side. He looked down at himself.

"I cannot even walk in these," he said. "I must take them off."

So he took them all off and laid them aside. "Where is my stick?" he said. "I will have that."

He took up his stick and walked off down to the brook. He chose five smooth round stones, and put them into the shepherd's bag that he carried. Then he took his sling in his hand and went boldly to meet the great giant Goliath.

How the giant mocked him! "Why do you carry a stick?" he shouted. "Do you think I am a dog that can be beaten?"

David ran quickly towards the giant. He put one of the smooth stones into his sling, then carefully he took aim, and flung the stone with all his strength at the laughing giant.

The stone flew straight through the air and hit Goliath right in the middle of his forehead, where he wore no armor. It sank in – and at once killed the giant.

He fell like a great tree, crashing to the ground, dead. David ran to him and snatched up his sword. He raised it and cut off the giant's head.

The enemy howled in fear when they saw that David had killed their giant hero, and fled away as fast as they could, with King Saul's men after them.

What a victory that was! How all the men crowded round the shepherd boy and sang his praises! The king sent for him and took him by the hand.

"Stay with me," he said. "Do not go back to your sheep. You shall be a captain in my army!"

So David stayed with Saul, and never again watched his father's sheep. He soon became a famous captain and won many battles for his king.

But the fight that he never forgot was the one with Goliath the Giant. One small round stone – and the victory was his!

Stories from the New Testament

The Night the Angels Came

It is Christmas night, and the carol singers are at the door. Bells are ringing joyfully, for Christmas is one of the happiest times of the year. How many Christmas nights have there been – yes, almost two thousand!

What happened on the first Christmas night of all? We will go to a little hilltop town and see.

Bethlehem was in darkness that first Christmas night, but it was not quiet. Many visitors had come to the little town, and it was full of people.

Two travelers came late that night. They were a man and wife – Joseph and Mary. Mary rode on a little grey donkey, and she was very tired. They came to an inn, and Joseph knocked on the door.

"We are full," said the innkeeper. "There is no room here – no room anywhere in Bethlehem tonight."

"No room at the inn! But my wife is very tired," said Joseph. "She must rest."

The innkeeper was sorry for the young woman on the donkey. "I will send my servant to a stable I have, and you may rest there when he has swept it and put down straw for you to lie on," said the man. "My oxen sleep there – it is the only place I can give you."

So Joseph took his wife, and the little donkey to the stable. It was only a cave in the hillside behind the inn, where big patient oxen stood, staring around in the light of the lantern.

Mary was glad to lie down in the straw. The wind blew into the cave and Joseph hung his cloak over the entrance to keep it out. The oxen made room for their little donkey. He was glad to be at rest too.

And that night the little Jesus was born to Mary – Jesus the son of God. Mary held him in her arms, and loved him.

She took long pieces of linen and wrapped the tiny baby in them, winding them around and around, for in those days they were a baby's first clothes, and were called swaddling-clothes.

There was no cradle for him. "Where can we put the child?" said Mary. "He must not lie in the straw."

"I will put some hay in the manger that the oxen eat from," said Joseph. "It shall be his cradle."

And so the baby was put in the manger, with soft hay to keep him warm. The little son of God, king of all the world, slept soundly there. No one knew that a great king had been born that night, no bells rang out for him, no one rejoiced at his birth but Joseph and Mary.

But up in heaven all the angels knew what a wonderful thing had happened. They rejoiced and longed to tell the great news. Whom should they tell? All that night they had watched over the sleeping town of Bethlehem, marveling to know that the little son of God had been born into this world of ours.

The town was silent and dark. No one was awake there to hear the great news – but wait, shepherds were awake on the quiet hillside outside the town. *They* should hear the news!

Yes, shepherds were there, watching their sheep, their dogs with them, guarding them from the fierce wolves that often roamed over the hills. They sat round a fire, for the night was cold, and they spoke of all the travelers they had seen going into Bethlehem that day.

And then a strange and wonderful thing happened. The sky suddenly became very bright, and a great light shone from it that lit up the whole of the hillside! The angels were coming to tell the wakeful shepherds the great news.

When the light shone round them, the shepherds looked
up fearfully, amazed at the brilliance. "What is this light
in the sky?" they wondered.

Then they saw a shining being in the middle of the

light – one of God's angels. The angel spoke and his voice came over the hillside like music.

The shepherds fell down on their knees and covered their faces, frightened and amazed. What was this? First a great light in the sky – then an angel, an angel who spoke in a mighty voice, and told them amazing news.

"Fear not!" said the angel, "for behold I bring you good tidings of great joy, which shall be to all people. For unto you is born this day a savior, which is Christ the Lord. And this shall be a sign unto you – you shall find the babe wrapped in swaddling-clothes and lying in a manger."

The shepherds listened. They raised their heads and gazed in awe at the shining angel with his great wings and his beautiful face. What was happening to them tonight?

Suddenly the sky disappeared, and a host of bright beings shone there, filling the night with radiance. Everywhere the shepherds looked they saw angels, angels who sang loudly and joyfully.

"Glory to God in the highest, and on earth peace, goodwill towards men."

The angels sang these words over and over again, and the shepherds listened and marveled. What a host of angels! What wonderful singing! The simple shepherds had never in their lives imagined anything so strange.

Then the dazzling light faded away. The darkness came back, and in the sky the stars shone again. The angels had gone.

The shepherds talked in low voices, amazed and fearful. "They were angels! And what news they brought! They said that a savior had been born to us in Bethlehem. Surely we must go to find him, this little king in a manger!"

And so the shepherds went to find the little Jesus. They were the only ones in the world who knew that he was born to Joseph and Mary. They came to the stable and peeped inside. By the light of the lantern there they saw the tiny baby in the manger, wrapped in swaddling-clothes, just as the angel had said!

Mary awoke when she heard the shepherds whispering at the entrance. She took her baby from the manger and held him in her arms – and all the shepherds came into the cave and knelt down before the little king to worship him.

They told Mary what the angels had said, and she

held her little child close, and wondered to hear their strange story. She looked down at her sleeping baby.

"Little Son of God!" she said. "You have only a manger to sleep in, with hay for a bed – but angels have come to sing of your birth!"

That was the first Christmas night, a night of wonder and joy. Angels do not sing on Christmas night now – *we* sing instead, and in our carols tell once again the wonderful story. Shepherds do not come to worship the little babe – but, instead, *we* pray, and rejoice as the angels did, that once, so long ago, the little king of the world was born.

When Jesus Was a Child

Joseph was a carpenter. He lived with Mary in a small white-washed house on a green hillside. The little Jesus grew up with all the other children around, and was very happy.

The little house was in the village of Nazareth in the land of Galilee. It was very much like all the other houses round. Joseph white-washed it each year, and Jesus helped him.

The little Jesus loved all the birds and animals around. He fed the pigeons, and brought water for the thirsty donkey which passed his house.

The little boy helped Joseph in his carpentry too. He grew up to the sound of hammering and sawing. Sometimes Joseph would call loudly for him. "Jesus! I need your help!"

Then the small boy would run to his father's shop and hold a piece of wood steady for him, or find the nails he needed.

He went out on the hillside with his mother, the gentle, loving Mary. How lovely the hills were in the spring and summer, spread with thousands of brilliant flowers, their scent blowing on the wind.

Jesus noticed everything. He loved to play with the lambs, he grieved when one was lost, he saw the sparrows building their nests, he watched the men at work in the fields, sowing seed as they walked up and down, or in summer-time cutting the corn.

He went to the well to fetch water for his mother, and listened to all the talk there, for it was a great meeting-place. The same well that Jesus fetched water from as a small boy is still to be seen today in Nazareth. How often did he gaze down into the clear water, and then fill his pitcher like all the other children?

His mother told him stories at night as yours does. He heard about Noah and how he made the great Ark, he listened to tales of the Giant Goliath, and of Daniel in the lion's den. He learned to pray.

He was gentle with animals, kind to his companions, loving to his parents. As he grew, he stored in his mind pictures of all the things he loved – the little lost lambs, the gleaming flowers, the first green blades of the corn, the seed that was scattered in the springtime, and grew in the fields . . . and all these things he put into his stories later on.

You are sure to hear some of them, for when he was a man he gathered the children round him and told them many many tales – he told them to grown-ups too, and we can read them in the Bible. When you hear them you will say: "How I wish I could have stood by his knee and heard him tell these tales to *me*!"

Satan Comes to Jesus

Jesus lived with his father and mother in the little white house for many years. He went to school with the other boys. Then he learned to be a carpenter, as his father was.

Jesus had plenty of time to think as he hammered and sawed and planed. He thought of the people he knew – some so kind, but others selfish and cruel, some just and merciful, and others unjust, spiteful, and mean. He knew good from evil, and he wanted to tell everyone that only goodness and kindness mattered. One day he must go out into the world and tell the people what he knew.

But Joseph died and Mary needed him, so he stayed with her. He would go when the right time came, but not till then.

At last the time came. "Now I must leave this city of Nazareth," said Jesus. "I must go and do the work that God my father in heaven has sent me to do. I must tell people to love one another; I will found a great kingdom of love and preach to all who will listen to me.

And so he left the little village he knew so well, and

went out into the world. He knew that he had been chosen by God to do his work, and he knew too that within himself was a great power – a strange gift that would help him to do things that no one else had ever done.

Jesus went into the lonely countryside so that he might think about what he was going to do. He meant to preach and to tell stories, to comfort and to heal. To found a kingdom of love was a great task. He must prepare for it and God would help him.

Someone was watching Jesus, someone who was very much afraid of his goodness and power. It was Satan, the Prince of Evil. What was this man Jesus planning to do?

"I will go to him and whisper in his ear, and put thoughts into his mind to turn him away from the good life he means to lead," thought Satan. "He has a

wonderful power within him, such as no man has had
before – the power to do miracles, to heal those who are
sick – yes, even to bring back to life those who are dead!
I will not let him use that power for good – he shall use it
for *me*, and do evil things."

He came to Jesus. Jesus had been wandering about
the countryside for days, forgetting even to eat, for his
thoughts had been long and deep.

Satan thought he would tempt Jesus to use his wonderful powers for himself. "See," he said, "there are
stones over there – stones which you can easily turn
into bread, for you have the power. You are hungry –

why do you not eat, son of God? It is easy."

But Jesus would not do what Satan told him. Then Satan, as if it were in a dream, took Jesus to the highest pinnacle of the holy Temple, far away in Jerusalem.

"See!" he said, "you are here, high above the great city. It is written in the Bible that angels shall have charge over the son of God to guard him – and are you not the son of God? Throw yourself down from here, for the angels will bear you up in their hands, lest you dash your foot against a stone! Thus will you prove to everyone that you are the great son of God, and your task will be easy."

But Jesus would not listen. He would not use his great powers to do foolish things. Then Satan tried once more.

He took Jesus to the top of a high mountain. In a single moment of time, he showed him all the great kingdoms of the world.

"Look!" said Satan. "What grand kingdoms, what great power shall be yours, if you work for me instead of God. Follow me, Jesus, work for me as most men do. You are only a carpenter's son, and preaching and prayer will never make you a king. But do what *I* bid you, and I will make you the greatest man in the world!"

Jesus was angered. He turned on Satan and spoke

sternly to him. "Get you behind me, Satan! I must worship the Lord my God, and him only must I serve!"

Then Satan gave a loud cry and fled away defeated. Joy filled the heart of Jesus – he had conquered Satan for ever. He could work for God now, and the Prince of Evil would never again come near him.

And then suddenly it seemed to Jesus as if angels were around him, helping him and caring for him, and he was glad.

Jesus Begins his Work

And now I must tell you how Jesus chose his friends, the disciples who would help him in his work. He could not do it all alone. He must teach others so that they too might go with him and teach and pray.

One day Jesus was standing beside the lovely Lake of Galilee, and he saw fishermen at work in their boats. They were two men he liked very much – Simon and Andrew. They were good fishermen, brothers to one another.

Jesus called to them across the water. "Come with me!" he said, "and I will make you fishers of men!"

The two brothers looked up and saw Jesus standing there. They had no idea what he meant by his words, they only knew that he had called them to come to him.

They pulled in their nets, and rowed to the shore. There was something about this man who had called to them that made them want to follow him to the end of the world.

Not far off were two other brothers, mending nets in a boat, with their old father. Jesus called across the water again.

"Come with me!"

And the two brothers came at once. Their names were John and James, and they loved Jesus as soon as they saw him.

These four were his first real friends and were close to him all his life. One of them, Simon, was a very lovable man. Jesus gave him a new name.

"I shall call you Peter," he said, "because Peter means a rock. I need a rock, Peter, on which to build my kingdom, and because I want your help, you shall be that rock."

Jesus chose eight more friends, and now he had twelve disciples, who followed him wherever he went. They were very happy together as they traveled about the countryside, and the twelve never ceased to marvel at the wonderful things that their master did and said.

Jesus was happy too. His great work had begun. He went from place to place, talking to all the people he met. He taught them about God, and about the kingdom of love. He spoke very simply, and everybody understood his words, even the children.

The boys and girls loved him. They knew he was good and kind. They clustered round his knees whenever he sat down, and listened to his words.

"Do good," Jesus told them. "Be kind. Love one

another, then happiness will come to you."

The people listened to him too, and like the children, they knew that here was a man who was goodness itself. They followed him about, and repeated his words to one another.

And then Jesus began to use his great gift of healing. He had always known that within himself he had a strange power. Now, by touching someone ill or in pain, he could heal them. Their illness left them, the pain vanished, they were well again!

Soon the whole countryside was talking about this wonderful healer. "He touched my child and her fever left her – she leapt from my arms and ran and danced!" said a mother.

"He spoke to my husband, who has lain ill on his bed for years," said a woman. "He told him to get up – and lo and behold, he stood up and walked. This man is from God, he is so kind and good."

"He heals both our souls and our bodies," said a man. "My mind and my ways were evil, my soul was sick –

but he has healed it, as he heals sick bodies. Surely this is our savior!"

And so it came about that wherever Jesus went the crowds followed him – some to hear, some to watch, some to be healed – and the children followed because they loved him with all their hearts.

A Little Boy Who Was Ill

Now I am going to tell you how Jesus once healed a little boy.

In the town of Capernaum there lived a nobleman. He had a small son, and his father loved him very dearly.

One day the little boy didn't want to play. He looked ill. His father took him on his knee and felt how hot his hands and head were. "I will call the doctor," said the nobleman.

The doctor came and ordered the little boy to bed. "He will soon be better," he said. But he was wrong. The child tossed and turned, moaning in pain, and became worse.

His father took him into his arms. "Send for other doctors," he said to his servants, but when they came, they shook their heads. "Your little boy is very ill," they said. "We can do nothing for him."

Then the nobleman knew that they thought his son was dying, and he went into his room to weep. What could he do for his little boy now? His servants heard him weeping and they went to him.

"Master," they said, "there is a wonderful healer called

Jesus. He is a very good man. Couldn't you get him here to your little boy?"

"Where is this man?" said the nobleman at once. "At the town of Cana, do you say? I will go to him and beg him to come to my boy."

The nobleman set off to Cana. This healer must come back with him, he must! If only he would heal his son he would give him anything he asked!

He came to Cana and tried to find out where Jesus was. "Where is this wonderful doctor?" he said.

"He is no doctor," said a man. "He is someone who preaches of goodness and love – and because he is so good he is able to heal bodies as well as souls."

"How shall I know him?" asked the nobleman. "By the beauty and goodness in his face," answered the man. "I will bring him to you. See, he is over yonder, talking of the love of God."

The nobleman went to the house, and waited inside for Jesus to come. He paced up and down. If only this man Jesus would come back to Capernaum with him!

Jesus came into the room – and at once the nobleman knew that here was someone he could trust, a man whose goodness looked out from his eyes, and who had great power to comfort and heal.

The nobleman went to him. "Sir!" he said, "my little boy is very ill, he is dying. Please come back with me and heal him. You can make him well again, I know you can. I love him so very much. Sir, will you come back with me?"

Jesus looked at the nobleman in his rich clothes. Had this man come just to see him do a miracle, as so many men came? How many many people had said: "If this man does a miracle before my eyes, then I will believe he is the son of God!" Jesus did not want people to believe in him just because he did miracles. He spoke to the nobleman.

"You and the others only want to see me do miracles," he said. "If I do something wonderful then you believe in me, but only then."

The nobleman gazed at Jesus in despair. "Sir, I have not come to see signs or wonders!" he said. "Indeed I have not. I have come only because my son is dying, and

I know you can cure him. But if we do not go now, he will die. Come with me, I beg of you!"

Jesus looked at the unhappy man, and he pitied him and loved him. "Do not fear," he said. "Your son lives. Go home now, and you will see I have spoken truly."

The nobleman gazed at Jesus, and believed him. He looked once again at that grave and beautiful face and then, his heart suddenly filling with joy, he ran from the house.

"He said that my boy lives! He has not seen him, he has not spoken to him nor touched him – and yet he has healed him. I know it in my heart, I know it!" The nobleman was so sure that his little son was better that he could hardly run fast enough for joy.

He came near his home. His servants were watching for him, and they ran to meet him, crying out joyfully.

"Your son is well, sir, he is well! See, he comes to meet you!"

Then the nobleman saw his little boy coming towards him, one of the servants holding him by the hand. He went down on one knee and held out his arms. The boy nestled into them happily.

"Where have you been, my father?" he said. "See, I'm better now. Aren't you going to play with me? My head doesn't hurt any more."

The nobleman stood up with his child in his arms, so joyful that at first he could not say a word. He smiled around at his servants, pressing the child close against him.

"Tell me," he said, "at what time did the child get better?"

"Sir," said a servant, "he seemed to be dying, and then, suddenly, at seven o'clock, the fever left him and he was quite better."

"At seven!" said the nobleman. "Yes – it was at seven, exactly at seven, that Jesus said to me: 'Your son lives.'

Truly he is a wonderful man. We will go to hear him preach. We will obey his commands. There is nothing that I will not do for this man Jesus!"

And from that time the nobleman and all his household loved Jesus and believed in his words. As for the little boy, he went to find him whenever he could, to hear his wonderful stories.

I will tell you some of the stories another time. You will like them as much as the little boy did who listened at his knee.